RAINBOWS AND HALOS

Stacy Allen

childsworld.com

Published by The Child's World®
800-599-READ • www.childsworld.com

Copyright © 2025 by The Child's World®
All rights reserved. No part of this book may be reproduced or utilized in any form or by any means without written permission from the publisher.

Photography Credits
Photographs ©: iStockphoto, cover, 1, 5; A. LaValle/National Park Service, 2–3; Lukas Jonaitis/Shutterstock Images, 6; Shutterstock Images, 7, 8, 14, 17; Baiterek Media/Shutterstock Images, 9; Elena Pimukova/Shutterstock Images, 11 (wavelengths); Albert Stephen Julius/Shutterstock Images, 11 (prism); Olga Donchuk/Shutterstock Images, 12; Red Line Editorial, 13; Jne Valokuvaus/Shutterstock Images, 16; J. Wei/National Park Service, 19; Chuck Elmore/Shutterstock Images, 21

ISBN Information
9781503894433 (Reinforced Library Binding)
9781503895171 (Portable Document Format)
9781503895997 (Online Multi-user eBook)
9781503896819 (Electronic Publication)

LCCN 2024942897

Printed in the United States of America

ABOUT THE AUTHOR
Stacy Allen writes poetry and nonfiction children's books. She saw a lot of rainbows as a kid when her family moved to Kailua, Hawaii.

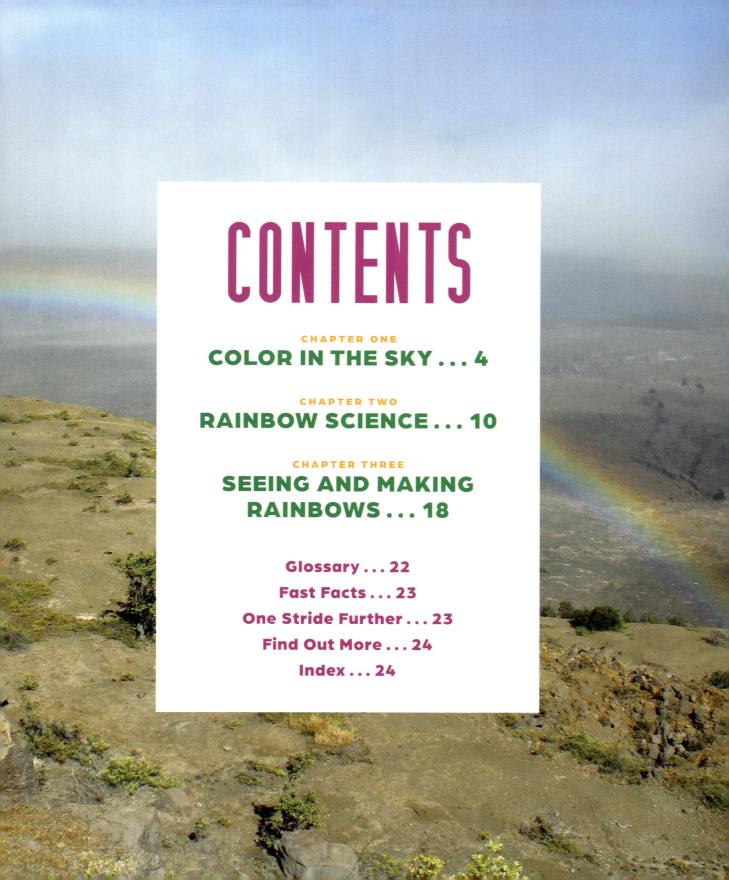

CONTENTS

CHAPTER ONE
COLOR IN THE SKY . . . 4

CHAPTER TWO
RAINBOW SCIENCE . . . 10

CHAPTER THREE
SEEING AND MAKING RAINBOWS . . . 18

Glossary . . . 22
Fast Facts . . . 23
One Stride Further . . . 23
Find Out More . . . 24
Index . . . 24

CHAPTER ONE

COLOR IN THE SKY

Oh no! Dark clouds are moving in. KJ and Sierra's dragon kite flies high above the beach. The kite's tail whips around wildly. Rain begins to fall. Sierra runs across the sand to help Dad with the towels. KJ starts to reel in the kite string. The kite dips low over the bay. It almost crashes into the waves! Then it rises again. KJ watches the kite. Raindrops land on his head and arms.

The color of the sky is changing. Behind KJ, the Sun is still shining. But behind the kite, the sky is dark blue. A huge rainbow appears over the water! KJ's shadow points to the very center of the rainbow's arc. He can see every color. Red is at the top. "Look!" KJ yells. "There's a rainbow!"

Sierra is far down the beach. She barely hears KJ yell. Then she turns to face the water. "Wow!" she says. "It's so beautiful!" Though she is standing far from KJ, Sierra seems to be looking at the center of the huge rainbow, too.

When the Sun shines during a thunderstorm, a rainbow can form.

OTHER RAINBOWS

FOGBOW

Fogbows are usually white. They are sometimes called ghost rainbows. Fogbows can be spotted on sunny but foggy days. Moonbows are rare nighttime rainbows. Sunlight bounces off the Moon and creates a pale rainbow. Red rainbows happen at sunset. When the Sun is lower in the sky, the cooler colors disappear. The rainbow appears completely red.

A rainbow is an image in the **atmosphere**. It can be seen. But it cannot be touched. Every rainbow needs two main ingredients. Sunlight is one. Clear water in the air is the other. The clear water could be raindrops or mist. The angle of the Sun is important, too. For KJ and Sierra, the conditions for a rainbow to appear are just right. The Sun is shining behind them. Rain is falling. The Sun is low in the sky.

There is only one rainbow in the sky. Yet KJ and Sierra each see it differently. This is because a rainbow looks different depending on where the viewer is standing. Sierra and KJ are not standing together. They each see the image projected through different raindrops.

EXTRA COLORS

Supernumerary means there is more than the usual number of something. Supernumerary rainbows have extra patterns of color repeating inside the arc of the primary rainbow.

Rainbows are shaped like circles. But on Earth, a rainbow looks like an arc in the sky. This is because of the **horizon**. People cannot see below the horizon. This means part of the rainbow is blocked.

There are many types of rainbows. A double rainbow has two arcs in the sky. The **primary** rainbow is brighter. The second rainbow appears above the primary rainbow, like a faded reflection.

Rainbows are not the only images that can appear in the atmosphere. A halo is a wide circle of light around the Sun or the Moon. Halos often appear white, but some halos have color. A halo does not need rain to appear. Halos form when light passes through ice crystals high in the clouds. Halos can even appear when there is a lot of dust or small particles in the air.

Halos can appear around the Moon as well as the Sun.

Rainbows seen from above are a full circle rather than an arc. This is because the horizon is not blocking the rainbow.

Rainbows and halos are considered some of the most beautiful images that occur in nature. They may seem magical, but they can be explained by science. Rainbows and halos appear when sunlight and water in the atmosphere interact in specific ways.

CHAPTER TWO

RAINBOW SCIENCE

A rainbow's colors are created by light. Light is energy that travels in waves. Most light is invisible to human eyes. The light humans can see is called the visible light **spectrum**. Each color has a different **wavelength**. Red waves are the longest. Violet waves are the shortest.

Visible light can be **refracted** into individual colors. This happens when light enters a **prism**. The surface of a round raindrop can refract sunlight, just like a prism can. The surface of the raindrop bends the light as it enters. The light hits the back of each raindrop and is reflected back out.

SCIENTISTS AND RAINBOWS

Scientists have been fascinated with rainbows for a long time. In 1637, René Descartes published a work that included Europe's first detailed study of rainbows. In the 1660s, Isaac Newton learned that white light can be separated by refraction in a prism. Newton recombined the colors by passing them through a prism again.

PRISMS AND WAVELENGTHS

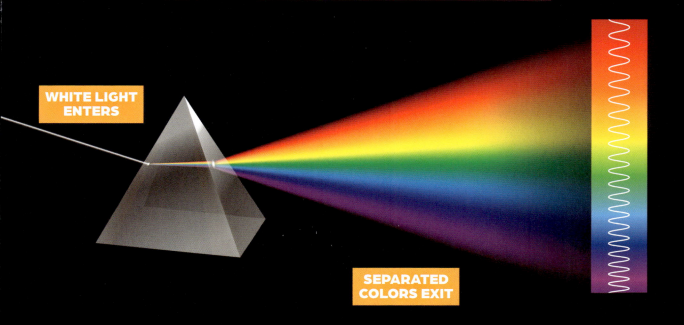

Visible light is a small part of the light spectrum. Other light wavelengths include ultraviolet light, infrared light, X-rays, and radio waves.

As the light leaves the raindrop, it is refracted again. Because of their different wavelengths, each color leaves the raindrop at a different angle. This creates the image of a rainbow in the sky.

The color spectrum appears arranged from longest to shortest wavelength. The order is always red, orange, yellow, green, blue, indigo, violet. The colors blend and blur together.

In a primary rainbow, red is always at the top of the curve. Violet is always at the bottom. In a double rainbow, the colors of the secondary rainbow are in the same order but reversed. The reds of the two rainbows face each other. The sky between the two rainbows appears darker than the sky above and below the rainbows. This is known as Alexander's Dark Band.

The secondary rainbow of a double rainbow is paler than the primary rainbow.

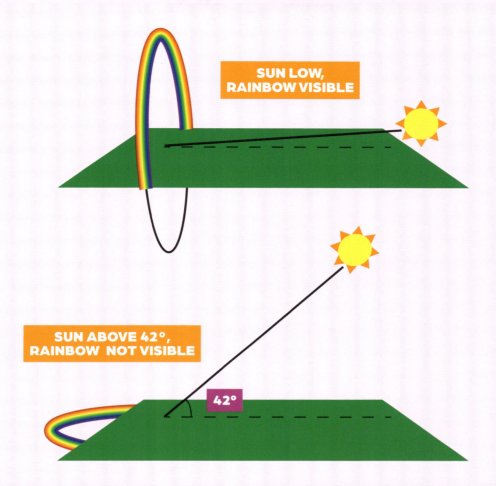

A rainbow and the Sun behave a little like opposite ends of a playground seesaw. The higher the Sun goes, the lower the rainbow goes, until the rainbow is below the horizon.

In order to see a rainbow, a person must be facing away from the sun while rain is falling. Rainbows occur only when the Sun is low in the sky. As the angle of the Sun increases above the horizon, the rainbow dips lower in the sky. Once the Sun rises to 42 degrees, the rainbow is no longer visible in the atmosphere. It is below the horizon, so the viewer cannot see it.

Sunlight refracts through thin, wispy clouds to create halos.

Halos are also formed by refraction of light. Halos are most likely to occur when there is a layer of thin, wispy **cirrus** or **cirrostratus** clouds in the sky. The ice crystals in these clouds can have a hexagon shape. They refract and reflect sunlight, creating halos. Halos around the Moon are also caused by sunlight. This is because the Moon does not make its own light. It reflects the light of the Sun.

The most common halos appear at the same distance from the Sun or the Moon. Scientists call these wide rings in the sky 22–degree halos. When light refracts inside ice crystals in the clouds, it bends at an angle of about 22 degrees.

Sun dogs are also called mock Suns or parhelia, which means "with the Sun."

The ice crystals in high cirrus clouds produce Sun dogs and fire rainbows. Sun dogs appear as spiky streaks or rounded bursts of light on either side of the Sun. They extend out from a halo. Sun dogs can have rainbow colors. They can also appear white. Sometimes Sun dogs are the only part of a halo that is visible.

Fire rainbows are rare and colorful, but they are not actually rainbows. They are horizontal rainbow-colored images that can look like flames in the sky. Both Sun dogs and fire rainbows are caused by refraction of sunlight through ice crystals.

Fire rainbows look like colorful clouds.

CHAPTER THREE

SEEING AND MAKING RAINBOWS

A rainbow can appear anywhere there is sunshine and rain. But some places are more likely to have rainbows than others. Rainbows occur frequently in Hawaii. This is because the weather in Hawaii can change quickly. Misty rain showers are often followed by bursts of sunlight and then more rain. These showers produce very small raindrops, which are better for creating rainbows. These weather patterns are caused by Hawaii's mountains and **trade winds**.

People can create rainbows, too. On a sunny day, people can stand with their backs to the Sun. They can spray water from a hose into the air. Covering part of the nozzle with a thumb turns the spray into a fine mist. Rainbow colors can appear in the mist.

Hawaii has been called the rainbow capital of the world. This double rainbow over the Uēkahuna Bluff was captured at Hawaii Volcanoes National Park.

Halos, Sun dogs, and fire rainbows can occur anywhere on Earth. Some types of halos occur only in places where the air is very cold. Halos may appear on days with high cirrus or cirrostratus clouds. They can also be seen in areas with lots of dust or ash in the air, such as areas with active volcanoes.

To see a rainbow, people have to be looking away from the Sun. But halos form around the Sun. Because viewers have to face the bright sunlight, halos are more dangerous to see. Looking directly at the Sun damages people's eyes. One way people can observe halos safely is to block the Sun. They can do this with their hands or by standing behind a building or a tree. To see where a halo forms, people can shade their eyes with one hand. Then they can stretch out their other arm and cover the Sun with their thumb. When they stretch out their pinky finger, the pinky points to the place where the halo will be. Though Sun halos can be dangerous, people can look directly at a Moon halo.

To increase their chances of seeing a rainbow, people can watch for the morning or late afternoon Sun shining when it rains. They can keep watch on the changing weather. To see halos, they can look for high, wispy clouds covering the sky. These all increase a person's chances of seeing a beautiful image in the atmosphere.

Rainbows can form in the mist of fountains, waterfalls, garden hoses, and more.

GLOSSARY

atmosphere (AT-muss-feer) An atmosphere is the layer of gases that surrounds a planet. Rainbows appear in Earth's atmosphere.

cirrostratus (seer-oh-STRAT-uss) Cirrostratus clouds are thin clouds high in the atmosphere that cover the sky like a veil. Halos can appear when sunlight passes through ice crystals in cirrostratus clouds.

cirrus (SEER-uss) Cirrus clouds are wispy, thin clouds made of ice crystals that are high in the atmosphere. When sunlight passes through ice crystals in cirrus clouds, Sun dogs may appear.

horizon (huh-RYE-zun) The horizon is the line where the sky and the Earth meet. Earth's horizon causes a rainbow to look like an arc rather than a full circle.

primary (PRY-mayr-ee) Something primary is the main or most important thing. The primary rainbow is the brightest rainbow in a double rainbow.

prism (PRIH-zuhm) A prism is a clear, solid object that bends a beam of white light and separates it into colors. Isaac Newton used a prism to separate the colors of the rainbow.

refracted (rih-FRAK-ted) When light is refracted, it passes through an object and changes appearance. Light refracted through raindrops can become a rainbow.

spectrum (SPEK-truhm) A spectrum is a range of something, such as color. Visible light is the spectrum of colors that humans can see.

trade winds (TRAYD WINDZ) Trade winds are winds that circle the Earth around the equator, blowing from east to west. Trade winds are part of why Hawaii has so many rainbows.

wavelength (WAYV-lenkth) A wavelength is the distance between two waves. The color red has the longest wavelength of the colors in the visible spectrum.

FAST FACTS

✹ A rainbow appears when the Sun is shining, rain is falling, and the angle of the Sun is low in the sky.

✹ Halos are formed when sunlight refracts through ice crystals in high clouds.

✹ Sun dogs are bursts of light that can be colorful. They appear on both sides of the Sun.

✹ Fire rainbows look like flames of color in the sky.

✹ Rainbows appear as arcs because of the horizon. Without the horizon, a rainbow would be a complete circle.

✹ Light is made up of waves. The colors in the visible light spectrum each have different wavelengths.

✹ Rainbow colors always appear in the same order, which is based on their wavelengths. The order is red, orange, yellow, green, blue, indigo, violet.

✹ Isaac Newton used a prism to prove that white light contains all the colors of the rainbow.

✹ Hawaii's weather conditions make it a place where people can see lots of rainbows.

ONE STRIDE FURTHER

✹ Have you ever seen a rainbow? If so, what kind did you see?

✹ Would you rather see a halo around the Sun or the Moon? Why?

✹ If you could rename Sun dogs and fire rainbows, would you? Why or why not? If so, what would you call them?

FIND OUT MORE

IN THE LIBRARY

Flint, Katy. *Nature's Light Spectacular*. Beverly, MA: Wide Eyed Editions, 2020.

Owens, L. L. *The Sun*. Parker, CO: The Child's World, 2025.

Roehrig, Artemis. *Rainbow Science: Discover How Rainbows Are Made with 23 Fun Experiments and Colorful Activities!* North Adams, MA: Storey Publishing, 2024.

ON THE WEB

Visit our website for links about rainbows and halos:

childsworld.com/links

Note to Parents, Caregivers, Teachers, and Librarians: We routinely verify our web links to make sure they are safe and active sites. So encourage your readers to check them out!

INDEX

Alexander's Dark Band, 12
angle of the Sun, 6, 13

clouds, 4, 8, 15–16, 19, 21
colors, 4, 6, 8, 10–12, 16–17, 18
creating rainbows, 18

Descartes, René, 10
double rainbows, 7, 12

fire rainbows, 16–17, 19
fogbows, 6

halos, 8–9, 15–16, 19–21
Hawaii, 18
horizon, 7, 13

moonbows, 6

Newton, Isaac, 10

prisms, 10–11

rainbows, 4–9, 10–13, 17, 18, 20–21
red rainbows, 6
refraction, 6, 8, 10–11, 15, 17

safely viewing halos, 20
Sun dogs, 16–17, 19